DIVORCE
AND YOUR FAMILY™

LIFE IN A
BLENDED
FAMILY

BECKY LENARKI AND JULIE LEIBOWITZ

ROSEN
PUBLISHING®

New York

Published in 2017 by The Rosen Publishing Group, Inc.
29 East 21st Street, New York, NY 10010

Copyright © 2017 by The Rosen Publishing Group, Inc.
First Edition

Library of Congress Cataloging-in-Publication Data

Names: Lenarki, Becky.
Title: Life in a blended family / Becky Lenarki and Julie Leibowitz.

Description: New York : Rosen Publishing, 2017. | Series: Divorce and your family| Includes index.
Identifiers: ISBN 9781508171294 (library bound)
Subjects: LCSH: Stepfamilies—Juvenile literature.

Classification: LCC HQ759.92 L45 2017 | DDC 306.874'7—dc23
Manufactured in China

CONTENTS

INTRODUCTION

Every Friday, Cherese and her twin brother, Michael, ride the bus to their father's house after school and stay until their mom picks them up on Sunday. Their father lives with his new wife, Gina, and their toddler, Austin. Cherese likes being there well enough, but she misses out on the Friday night football games and other social activities because she has to go to her dad's. Her dad usually goes into the office for a few hours over the weekend, so she and Michael are left with Gina and Austin for some of the time. Sometimes she wonders why she and Michael go there at all if their father doesn't want to spend time with his old family.

When they get home on Sunday, Cherese and Michael have to rush to do their homework because they can't get it done with Austin in the way. They live with their mom and stepfather, George. George's son, Nick, sometimes stays there when he's home from college. He doesn't seem to want to spend much time with Cherese or Michael, but when he does he's cool.

Holidays are a production. They trade off on Thanksgiving—one year with Mom and George, the next

Blended families have become increasingly more common in our society. While adjusting to a new parent and siblings can be awkward, there are many rewards to being part of a blended family.

year with Dad and Gina (and Austin). They always spend Christmas Eve and Christmas Day with Mom and George, with Christmas dinner at their grandparents' house. The day after Christmas, their dad picks them up and they have a second Christmas with his family. It's fun to watch Austin as he gets more into Christmas, but Gina fawns over him while Cherese and Michael feel ignored.

Cherese feels like she has a lot of people in her family, but she's not sure how she fits in. She knows other kids who have blended families and they feel the same way. Sometimes she doesn't feel at home anywhere.

Are you part of a blended family? A blended family is made up of various combinations of parents, stepparents, siblings, stepsiblings, and half siblings. According to a 2011 report by the Pew Research Center, 42 percent of American adults have a step-relative. That means more than one-third of Americans have a stepparent, stepchild, or step or half sibling. And that doesn't include American children, 5 million of whom are stepchildren.

If you are a member of the growing number of blended families, you are probably aware of the challenges—and rewards—that are particular to this type of family. Learning to be part of a blended family is often extremely difficult. It is even more difficult if you are adjusting during the already challenging teen years. You are going through so many changes already, and you are starting to separate yourself from your parents and family and seek your own identity. These changes are complicated by having to adapt to the dynamics of a new family. You wonder where you fit in.

This resource will examine the roles that stepparents and stepsiblings play in your life. It will discuss the feelings you might be experiencing regarding your new family. You may be very angry or sad, and it is OK to feel that way. If your natural parents are divorced or you have experienced the death of a parent, you will certainly have all kinds of emotions and concerns about new parents and about new families. Most important, though, this resource will explain how to see the benefits of a blended-family situation. You will learn that blended families can be just as wonderful as natural families. In today's society, blended families are not unusual. Like any task, living in a blended family takes work. However, if you make the effort and the other family members do as well, your blended family can be a positive part of your life.

CHAPTER ONE

ENTERING A BLENDED FAMILY

After your parents divorce, you go through a lot of changes. For instance, you have to adapt to not living with one of your parents at any given time. After a while, you will get used to living with just one parent and having to shuttle back and forth between two homes.

But what happens when one or both of your parents get married? This may be something you're not prepared for. Or it may have been in the works and you've already gotten to know your future stepparent quite well. Either way, the person your parent is marrying will become part of your family, as will any children he or she brings to the new marriage. Maybe your parent and stepparent will even have a child together. This is what is known as a blended family.

A Difficult Adjustment

When you find out that one of your parents will be getting married again, you may have many different emotions. You will probably be upset that your parent has fallen in love with someone else.

It can be difficult to watch your parent remarry and have a child with that new spouse. You may feel left out of the family because you are not biologically related to the rest of the family.

You may wonder why he or she loves this person more than your other parent. You may be angry and think that this new person is trying to take the place of your other parent. Perhaps you are an only child who is living alone with a single parent, and you fear that your stepparent will ruin that special relationship you have with your natural parent. In any case, it is very difficult for a teen-ager to watch a parent enter into a marriage with someone new.

Approximately 75 percent of divorced people remarry, making it fairly likely that if your parents are divorced, one or both of them will get married again. If this happens, you must adjust to having a stepparent and perhaps stepsiblings, who are the children of your parent's new spouse. If you are living with the new family, your daily life will certainly change. You may have to share a room with a stepsibling. You may resent your stepparent for

When a parent remarries, you may acquire new stepsiblings along with your stepparent. You will have an easier transition to building a new family if you accept that your parent is much happier.

living in the same house as you, a constant reminder that your natural parents live in separate places. Will you still be able to spend time alone with your natural parent? Who will make the rules? Many questions will arise during the formation of the new family.

If your parents are divorced, you are probably still hoping that they will get back together someday. This is a rare event, however, and many kids have difficulty when a parent announces remarriage, mainly because it is a sign that the relationship between the parents is truly over. Trying to accept the situation and move on is the best way to handle it. It is definitely not easy, though, and no one expects you to warm up to the situation right away. But if you think of it in the sense that your life will be better without the tension of your parents' anger toward one another, and that your parents will certainly be happier— and nicer to be around—if they are not living together, you may find that divorce was the best thing.

Entry into a blended family as a teenager is significant in several ways. First, because you are at an age where you are mature enough to be aware of your surroundings and the changes within them, you understand exactly what is happening when your parent remarries. This is good because your parent is made to treat you as an adult and give you all the facts. You are too old for him or her to ignore you or "pull one over on you," as may be the case with much younger children. Also, you are at an age where you are intellectually able to reason and rationalize the situation. Although this is true, that does not necessarily mean that it is easy to listen to the voice of reason and accept your parent's remarriage. That takes a lot of courage, a lot of work, and a lot of time. As a result, this difficult time may be the most important period of growth that you will experience in your life.

REMARRIAGE AFTER THE DEATH OF A PARENT

When a parent has died, it is also difficult to cope with the remarriage of the living parent. You have had to deal with the loss of someone very close to you, and then you must acclimate to living with the person who is filling that role in your life. This is typically a very troubling situation for teens, as they experience a wide variety of emotions. Perhaps they are angry at the living parent for remarrying, and maybe they think that the living parent is trying to "replace" the parent who has died.

It is not that it is more difficult to cope with a blended family if you have experienced the death of a parent as opposed to divorce; it is simply a different set of factors. Unfortunately, the parent who has died is never coming back, whereas in the case of divorce, both of the parents are still alive. The finality of death may become more obvious when a parent remarries and may make it harder to accept the person your parent is marrying. On the other hand, maybe you like your new stepparent but feel that by doing so you are betraying the memory of the parent who died. You need to know that it is possible to like your stepparent and still lovingly remember your parent who has passed away. There is room for both.

Talk About It

Both of Franny's parents got married within a year of each other. She had just gotten used to her new life as a kid of divorce, and now a lot more changes were underfoot. Suddenly there were two houses, a stepmom and a stepdad, and three stepbrothers. Franny felt lost in the shuffle and didn't know where she fit in. She knew there were kids at school with two families, but she didn't know them well. None of her close friends understood how she felt. Even she wasn't sure how she felt! It was nice to see both of her parents happy, but she didn't like being left out.

Franny finally opened up to her art teacher one day after school when she was collecting her pottery from the kiln. Her art teacher said she understood because she was in a blended family herself. She had stepchildren from her husband's first marriage. Franny felt a lot better being able

Talking about how you feel can help you identify your emotions and make sense of why you feel them. You can seek the guidance of a counselor, teacher, minister, or even a friend who has been through the experience.

to express herself, and she learned a lot about what her parents were going through from her art teacher's stories about her own experience.

If you are in the position of trying to accept your parent's remarriage and you are confused and overwhelmed, know that you are not alone. Second marriages and stepfamilies are so common in today's society that many other teens are in the same situation. You can work your way through it with the help of your family or those outside the family, such as friends or school counselors.

The best way to address all types of blended-family situations is through communication. Family roundtable discussions are a good way to get to know the members of the family. Through these, you can talk about each person's feelings and needs, as well as the rules of the new family. Also, talk directly to your natural parent about the feelings and emotions you are experiencing so that he or she can try to help guide you through your adjustment. Remember, it is an adjustment for your parents, too.

CHAPTER TWO

THE NEGATIVE STEREOTYPES OF A BLENDED FAMILY

Remember how in fairy tales there was often a wicked stepmother who made the heroine's life miserable? Cinderella had to stay home from the ball to scrub floors, while her stepsisters got to have fun. In real life, stepparents and stepsiblings aren't usually so bad. You may think your stepdad hates you, but he doesn't. Like you, he is just trying to adjust to his new living situation.

Stepmothers Aren't Wicked

Jada could not believe it. Her father had just told her that he was going to marry Roberta, the woman he had been dating for the past year. Roberta was nice, but Jada did not understand why they had to get married. Now Roberta was going to be around all of the time. Jada would not be able to go over to her father's house and spend time just with him anymore. Now Roberta would be there, and so would her two kids, who were only in first grade and third grade. Whenever they were all together, no one paid any attention to Jada because Roberta's kids could not do anything by themselves.

Jada told her friend Johnny that her father was going to marry Roberta. "Oooh," Johnny said, "you're going to have a wicked stepmother! I wonder what she's going to do to you! Are you going to be able to play in the soccer game on Saturday? She might make you stay home and scrub the floor." Jada had not thought about that, but it was true, just like in a fairy tale. Stepmothers were always mean. Jada was very upset. She would probably never be able to play on the soccer team again.

It's not unusual to assume your new stepmother is going to be wicked. You probably grew up reading fairy tales, and you may believe the negative stereotypes created by these stories are real.

In *Cinderella* there was a wicked stepmother and evil stepsisters. These characters are what most teenagers think of when they picture being part of a stepfamily, so from the start, teens have a distorted perception of how their stepfamily will work. It is because of this misconception that you must try harder and harder to do away with these stereotypes.

It is important to understand that the stereotypes from these fairy tales are not universally true. Just because your parent is getting remarried does not mean that your stepparent will take an instant dislike to you and force you to lead a miserable life, nor will your stepsiblings taunt you and make you their slave. The fact that you are an important person in your parent's life

Not all stepmothers are wicked like the character in *Cinderella*. Most stepparents want to get to know you and love you because they love your parent. Make an effort to try to get to know the person your parent is marrying.

will make you an important person in your stepparent's life, and because of that, he or she will want to develop a good relationship with you.

Your New Siblings

The same misconceptions about stepparents are often associated with stepsiblings, too. In the beginning, although things may not be quite as easy as television shows such as *The Brady*

You may find yourself sharing a room with a stepsibling when your parent remarries. While this will be an adjustment and you might not always like it, it can work out if you set ground rules and show respect.

Bunch portray, odds are you will not be in a Cinderella situation either. Adolescence is one of the most difficult times in life to have to start living with brand-new people, particularly if other teens are involved. Everyone's emotions are heightened, and as a teenager, the last thing you want is to deal with somebody else's changes, confusion, or mood swings. You have enough to handle in your own life.

Just as your stepparent is going to play an important role in your life, so are your stepsiblings. After all, your parents have gotten married, and now you are all part of the same family. As we mentioned earlier, you may end up sharing a room with a stepsibling, putting you in very close quarters. In any case, try to consider your stepsiblings as positive factors in your new blended family. A stepsibling is a kid just like you, trying to fit into a new family.

In fact, a stepsibling can simply be a friend. If you are close in age, this is even more likely to happen. You might be surprised to find that it is nice to have a stepsibling around, a peer you can talk to—either in addition to your natural siblings or as a sibling you never had.

New Additions

At some point in time, your blended family may expand even more if your parent and stepparent decide to have a child together. Since you will have one common natural parent, this child will be your half sibling. For teenagers especially, it is difficult to have a new baby in the house. A baby causes many lifestyle changes for parents and families. As a teenager, it is one more massive change to cope with at a time that is already filled with transformations.

YOU ARE NOT ALONE

Remember one thing about adjusting to your blended family: you're not in it alone! Even if you are an only child and your parent marries someone without children, there are still three of you trying to adapt to a new situation. Most likely your parent and stepparent are figuring things out as they go along. They understand it's a difficult time for you, and it will help if you understand it's a difficult time for them, too.

If you have new stepsiblings, you already have one thing in common. Don't be afraid to tell them how you're feeling and encourage them to share their emotions with you. You're the only ones who are sharing the exact same experiences.

Having a new baby enter the family also stirs up many emotions. You may feel jealous of all the attention the baby gets or annoyed at how helpless he or she is. It is particularly hard to deal with the new baby if you come from divorced parents. The baby may be a strong sign of the existence of your stepfamily and the fact that your natural parents are not together anymore. However, ultimately the baby is your brother or sister, a bond that cannot be broken or ignored.

Although from a teenage perspective, it is very hard to identify with a new child, try to understand the baby's needs and think of him or her in a more positive way. If your parent and stepparent ask you to help take care of the baby or perform other chores related to the family, be flattered. It means that you

A new half brother or half sister can throw off the balance of the new family that you've just adjusted to. But it can also bring your family closer together. You can be a part of your new half sibling's life.

are independent and responsible enough to be trusted with your new brother or sister, as well as with other jobs that may make daily life in your household run a little smoother. It is a big step toward adulthood.

How Do You Fit In?

As a teenager, you are experiencing many changes. Aside from the standard physical changes of growth, you are also encountering psychological changes. You are slowly becoming an adult, one who is able to make his or her own decisions and who is forming a distinct personality. It is at this point in your life that

You may find yourself wanting to spend more time with your friends when you become a teenager, particularly if things are different or difficult at home. But family is important, too. You will have them the rest of your life.

you begin to separate from your parents and family and become an individual with your own thoughts and beliefs.

These changes are hard enough to deal with on their own, but if you are trying to adjust to a blended family at the same time, they are even more difficult. Just as you are trying to separate from the family and formulate a strong identity, you are simultaneously being pulled into this new group, the blended family, and depended upon to help make it work.

If you are in junior high or high school, you have only a few years or so before you go off to college or get a job, move out of your house, and become more independent. These possibilities may make it even harder to focus on being a part of your blended family. It is as though you are growing up and learning to interact with your family all over again while striving toward pursuing personal goals and leading a more autonomous life. It is a challenge, but you can do both. You can still be your own person while being a part of your blended family.

CHAPTER THREE

ADAPTING TO YOUR BLENDED FAMILY

W hen you're a teenager, you become used to change. Your body changes; your emotions change. Your relationship with your family and friends may change. It's not easy adding another change to all this. But change is a big part of entering a blended family. Suddenly, you might not feel like you fit in anymore. Your role in the family may change. How will you cope with such change?

Bridget and her dad had always been very close. Ever since her mom died ten years earlier, it had just been the two of them. But recently her dad had married Lee Ann, a woman with two sons. Lee Ann had been in the picture for a couple of years, but Bridget's dad hadn't brought her around much. And Bridget barely knew Lee Ann's sons.

That's why it was so difficult when they all moved in to the same house. Suddenly, Bridget didn't feel like she could walk into her dad's room to talk whenever she wanted to because Lee Ann might be there. And Bridget couldn't adjust to Lee Ann's sons, who were always wrestling

There is no doubt about it: your life will change in significant ways when you become part of a blended family. The adjustment will be much easier if you figure out your role in your new family.

around on the ground and having friends over for pizza. Bridget was used to a quiet life, and now she couldn't find peace anywhere.

And she felt completely alone because everyone else seemed to be adjusting just fine. Her dad played basketball with her stepbrothers in the driveway, and sometimes

One of the hardest things to deal with in life is change. Change can be scary, but it can also lead to wonderful things. Understanding that your life is changing is the first step toward making a positive adjustment.

Lee Ann even joined in. Bridget didn't like sports. No one seemed to be interested in what she liked to do. Even when Lee Ann tried to take her shopping or to a movie, Bridget felt strange. She wished she could have her old life back.

Coping with Change

While your blended-family life may present some drastic changes from the way your life was before your parent remarried, it is to your benefit to try to cope with those changes in a positive way. This can be hard, since you may not be all that happy about your parent's remarriage.

However, making the best of things can only make your life, and the rest of the family's, more comfortable. Whereas before perhaps you used to walk the dog and take out the garbage, maybe now your responsibilities have changed, so you do the dishes instead. The parents should be able to decide what responsibilities each child should have so that everyone feels comfortable.

Feeling comfortable, though, is not always so easy. It is a natural part of growing up to feel scared and insecure during adolescence, unsure of who you are and where you fit in. Most teens desperately want to conform to some kind of standard—to be like everyone else, to be cool. Teenagers in blended families often feel excessive pressure. They are trying to make sense of their new family structure and may think of it as another difference that sets them apart, out of the "cool" loop.

In addition to the list of normal developmental tasks, teens in blended families have extra challenges to master. Perhaps you have just started middle school, you are trying out for a sports team, and your first school dance is coming up in a few weeks.

One of your parents has just gotten remarried, and you suddenly have three stepbrothers. That is a lot to deal with all at once! Take a deep breath and relax.

Adolescence is all about growth and change, and coping with blended families is just one more challenge for teens to face. It might not be easy, but it will undoubtedly make you stronger and enable you to handle just about anything that comes your way.

Finding Your Role

Fitting in is a big part of teenage life. Most teens yearn to fit in at school, to make a place for themselves in a particular group, and to be popular with their peers. The same ideas apply when considering how a teen fits into his or her blended family. Roles in blended families may not be as clear as they are in natural families. You may not be quite sure what your place is and what your responsibilities are. You may be unhappy about your parent's remarriage, which makes settling into a blended family even harder.

Often your role in the typical family is somewhat structured by birth order: The oldest is the caretaker, and the youngest is the "baby" and is usually the most coddled. Middle children, generally, have a harder time finding their place in the family, as their position in the birth order does not give them a definitive role.

In any case, no matter what the birth order of your natural family, your role in the blended family will differ. Maybe you are now the babysitter for younger stepsiblings instead of being the youngest child, or perhaps you now have siblings when before

You may find that your role in your blended family is quite different from the role you are used to. If you were always the "baby" of the family, you might enjoy being a role model to younger siblings in your blended family.

you were an only child. Your role will carve itself out as time progresses. The responsibilities you had prior to your parent's remarriage may become greater, or they may become even less if there are now more people to share in the duties. You might try to think of this as one of the positives of your blended family.

Don't Become Isolated

Just as most teens worry about fitting in, they also worry about being excluded from a group or activity in a social setting. Once again, this applies to the blended-family situation as well. The way family members relate to each other depends on each person's personality. Perhaps you are quiet and shy, whereas your new stepparent and stepsiblings are more outspoken and aggressive. This may cause you to feel uncomfortable around them and prompt you to withdraw from the group.

It is important to realize in a situation like this that no one is excluding you on purpose. You just

If you are having trouble connecting with the new members of your family, an activity like a game, sport, craft, or cooking can help bring you together. In time, you will begin to understand and accommodate your differences.

have different characteristics that may take some getting used to, and the same goes for the rest of the family. Learning to accept other people's differences is something you will certainly have to do in order to help make the blended family work.

Getting yourself involved in family activities is extremely helpful in your adjustment. It is true that if you are indeed shy and have trouble in group situations, this may be hard. However, if you are simply withdrawing because you are angry about your parent's remarriage, you are only making your situation worse. You are letting your resentment and hostility toward the situation prevent you from making the best of things, and you will only find yourself more excluded and isolated. You will also be missing out on what could be a fun, enjoyable family situation. The more involved you are with the family, the more comfortable you will begin to feel in the group and the more you will fit in.

CHAPTER FOUR

GETTING OVER BAD BLOOD

Becoming a blended family isn't just about change. There are a lot of emotions involved. Even though you dealt with a lot of different feelings when your parents got divorced, many more will surface when a parent remarries. Be prepared for jealousy, hurt feelings, anger, and resentment.

Danny didn't like Fred, the guy his mother decided to marry. Fred was grumpy, and he barely talked to Danny. Danny didn't understand why his mother would rather be married to Fred and not his father. Danny certainly didn't feel the same way. He hated the idea that pretty soon Fred would be living in their house and sitting in Danny's father's chair. Danny wanted his father to move back into the house and be with his mother again.

When You Resent Your Stepparent

As you begin to deal with your new stepparent and his or her role in your life, it is natural to feel some hostility and resentment.

Life can be miserable when you don't like your stepparent. You might think your stepparent is mean or that he or she doesn't like you. Or you might resent your stepparent for taking the place of your parent.

After all, he or she is acting in the role of the parent who no longer lives with you. It is difficult enough to come to terms with the fact that one parent no longer lives in your house, so coping with a new person taking his or her role in the family is not easy.

You may also resent the fact that your natural parent now relies upon a new spouse for certain things, whereas before your parent may have relied upon you. It is as though the responsibilities you took on are no longer needed. This is very common in the case of an only child, in which a unique bond exists between the parent and child because it is just the two of them together.

When You Feel Guilty for Liking Your Stepparent

On the other hand, things may become even more confusing if you actually like your stepparent and begin to develop a relationship with him or her. You may feel that you are hurting your absent parent by being friendly with this new person; you feel disloyal. It is similar to the feeling you may have experienced if your parents are divorced, and while spending time with one parent you feel disloyal to the other.

FAVORITISM

When you inherit stepsiblings as a result of your parent's marriage, there can be plenty of conflicts. Just like brothers and sisters fight from time to time, so will stepbrothers and stepsisters.

During a fight, if your parent seems like he or she is taking the side of your stepsibling, don't get upset. Sometimes parents take it easy on their stepchild so that the stepchild won't feel threatened. In doing this, it may seem like your parent is being unfairly hard on you. If this happens, talk to your parent about how you felt betrayed. Chances are, he or she didn't do it intentionally.

Eventually, your parent will feel comfortable punishing your stepsiblings. But that also means that your stepparent will be comfortable punishing you. It's only fair!

However, as time goes on, you will learn that it is OK to like your stepparent; in fact, if you live with your stepparent, it will certainly make everyone's lives much easier if the two of you do get along. After a while, as you continue to grow and mature, you may even realize that by getting along with your stepparent, you have helped to create a new, harmonious family. If your parents are divorced and all you can remember of their marriage is tension and fighting, then the success of your blended family will definitely be a positive influence on your well being.

"Mom" or "Stepmom"?

An important issue that arises when we talk about feelings toward a stepparent is the name. What are you supposed to call your stepparent? There are a variety of options, and you must do what feels comfortable in your particular situation.

Most likely, calling your stepparent "Mom" or "Dad" will not work. Those names symbolize a kinship you established with your natural parents at birth, and they probably will not seem appropriate with anyone else.

Once again, though, every stepfamily situation is unique. Perhaps your father has died, and the man your mother is marrying plays an important part in your life. You may want to call him "Dad." It all depends on what the relationship is.

For teenagers, however, being on a first-name basis with their stepparent is the most common scenario. It helps create a casual, warm environment where you can think of your stepparent as your friend. It is important to remember that your stepparent is not a replacement for your parent who no longer lives with you; he or she is simply another parent, an "extra."

Express Yourself

Coping with all of these issues and emotions can be trying. Although you are on the path to adulthood, you are not there yet, and attempting to face these issues is a lot to handle all by yourself. You can, of course, talk to your parents. However, many teens find it helpful to talk to someone else, an outsider—someone whom you trust and who can be objective, who can help you wade through the tough issues you are facing, and who can try to make sense out of some of them.

There are many people like this who can help you: school psychologists, social workers, and community leaders are just some of them. Talking can really help, particularly if you are dealing with both social issues and family issues. You may be surprised

It's perfectly fine to like your stepparent. In fact, it's great! Developing a positive relationship with your stepmother or stepfather does not mean that you have stopped loving your natural mother or father.

at how a fresh view on things can make the situation a little clearer.

Another outlet that can be a great help in coping is a support group. You may have heard of adult support groups such as Divorced Dads or Parents Without Partners. These are groups that help adults deal with the issues that have affected their lives, such as divorce or the death of a spouse. There are groups like this for teens as well. You may find one right in your own school, run by a teacher or a school social worker. You may also find them in community centers or at the office of a psychologist.

For several reasons, this type of group can be helpful in coming to terms with the issues you are dealing with as a teenager. First, it is often

Joining and attending a support group can be a helpful way to adapt to living in a blended family. There, you will share your stories and hear the experiences of others who are in your situation.

easier to talk about problems in a group setting, where everyone has experienced similar life changes and can identify with your feelings. In a group that focuses on the remarriage of parents and on blended families, you may find it useful to hear other teens' stories and how they are coping. It may give you some ideas on how to adjust to your own situation. The group can also be a good outlet through which to express your anger, sadness, or whatever you are feeling to people who will listen and sympathize.

Staying Out of Your Parents' Issues

Jermaine's dad had recently married Sheila. Jermaine spent every weekend at their house and actually really liked Sheila. He had been scared at first, after hearing so many stories from his friends about bad stepmothers and how mean they were. But Sheila was different. She did not try to tell Jermaine

what to do or act like his mother. She was just very nice and seemed as though she wanted to be Jermaine's friend. One weekend, Jermaine's father had to work on Saturday. Jermaine was upset because they had made plans to go play laser tag. However, he still got to go: Sheila took him, and they had a great time. Then they met his father later for tacos.

When Jermaine came home from his father's house on Sunday evening, his mother asked how the weekend was and what he did. When Jermaine told her how Sheila had taken him out because his dad had had to work, Jermaine's mother spit out, "That's typical. Your father can never follow through on his promises. Always has to have someone else bail him out."

Jermaine got very upset when his mother said that. This was not the first time she had made a rude comment about his father that was not true. He really did not want to hear comments like that anymore. But he couldn't admit to his mother that Sheila was actually really cool and that he enjoyed spending time with her.

Just as you may be resentful or jealous of your stepparent for the role that he or she is trying to play or the fact that this person has diverted some of your parent's attention, be aware that your natural parent may actually feel the same way about your other parent's new spouse.

The previous scenario is a typical reaction of a mother's jealousy toward her child's stepmother. Jermaine's mother suddenly

Successfully adapting to a blended family means staying out of your parents' isssues. If they feel angry or hurt because you are fitting in to your new situation, it is not because of anything you did wrong.

felt threatened by her son's stepmother, who was acting more like a friend than a parent, and was afraid that Jermaine enjoyed spending time with her more than he enjoyed spending time with his own mother. As a defense mechanism, Jermaine's mother lashed out at his father. She really should just be happy that Jermaine was happy.

One of the biggest difficulties for a teen whose parents are divorced is the fact that he or she is often constantly being pulled back and forth between the parents. It is very hard for the parents to put the child's needs ahead of their own anger and resentment toward each other. The parents frequently start to bad-mouth each other in front of the child, and they may also criticize a step-parent, especially if it seems as though the child is developing a good relationship with this person.

If you are in this situation, do not be afraid to talk to your parent when he or she makes comments about your other parent that make you upset. Often if parents know how much this behavior is bothering their child, they will realize that they are simply being selfish and are making an already rough situation even worse. As we mentioned earlier, it is important for teens to realize that it is OK to like their stepparent.

Sometimes it is just hard for a parent to see his or her child forming a bond with a stepparent, particularly when it is the new spouse of a former spouse. Just as you may need reassurance from your parent that he or she is not being "taken away" by your new stepparent, your natural parent may need reassurance from you that he or she isn't being replaced either.

CHAPTER FIVE

THE HARD WORK OF A BLENDED FAMILY

One important element in adjusting to your blended family is time. No one expects you to come together as a happy family right away. You will need time to get to know and trust one another. Loving them as family members might take a while.

You loved the family you were born into without even thinking about it. This is called unconditional love. This is because you developed a bond with your parents and siblings—and they with you—from your earliest breaths. Since that isn't possible with your new family, you will have to work a little harder.

Finding Common Ground

When Soo-Hee and her mother first moved in with Todd, her stepfather, and his kids, Jake and Ethan, she felt very out of place. This wasn't the house she grew up in, and she wasn't used to sharing a bathroom with anyone, let alone two strange boys. At dinner, Todd and Soo-Hee's mother would try to ask all the kids about their day, but no one wanted to talk much.

Five years later, things are com-pletely different. Soo-Hee can't believe there was ever a time when she didn't have her two stepbroth-ers in her life. When Jake goes off to college next year, she will miss him terribly. And Todd has done so much for her over the years, like coach-ing her softball team and teaching her how to ski on their annual fam-ily trip to the mountains. She loves Todd, Jake, and Ethan like the fam-ily members that they are.

Getting used to your new blended family is no easy task, but bear in mind that it is probably not easy for any of the other family members either. Just as you need time to adjust to your new stepparent and/or stepsiblings, they need time to adjust to you. It takes a lot of effort on everybody's part to make the blended family work.

There are several things a blended family can do to help guide them through the rough spots of creating their family dynamic, and one of these things is to identify what they have in common. Members of blended families have all experienced significant losses. If the family members mourn their losses together, it will help them

One way to make a blended family work is to focus on the things you have in common. Even if you are very different, you have at least one thing in common: you all are trying to fit in to a blended family!

overcome grief and simultaneously form new bonds with one another.

As a teenager, if your parents are divorced, you may feel great sadness about it, and you may think that nobody can understand what you are going through. However, if you now have stepsiblings who also went through divorce, try talking to them about your experiences. You may be surprised to find that they are probably feeling the same emotions of grief and anger, and talking about these reactions to one another can help you not to feel so alone.

Work Together

Blended families must also develop new skills and learn how to make decisions as a group. At first it may seem strange, but with the guidance of the parents, the family will begin to form its own identity. Change is a major factor in the formation and success of a blended family. Once the members of the family all come to terms with the situation and begin to work together as one unit, instead of two, the blended family can be considered a real family, not a forced unification.

Have your parents get everyone together for a family meeting so that each member can openly discuss his or her thoughts and ideas. Your parents and other siblings may be just as anxious as you about where they stand in the family structure, and you may be surprised at how getting together to talk about fears and anxieties can prove to be quite helpful.

You must also be open to compromise. Try to accept new ideas and ways of doing things that may differ from the ways you used to do them. Give new ideas a chance before you dismiss them simply because "that's not the way we used to do it." One of the biggest obstacles blended families face is that they have limited shared family histories or shared ways of doing things, and they may have very different beliefs. If you can try to be open to new circumstances and responsibilities within the family, new traditions will arise.

Talk with a Family Counselor

In many cases, it is easier for blended families to work through their transition with the help of a counselor. If you have already seen a counselor on your own, you know the benefits of expressing your feelings to a professional therapist. This may help on a group basis as well, by bringing the entire family to counseling sessions to talk out any problems. Again, an objective listener can be a great asset.

Not only will a counselor lend an unbiased ear, but he or she will also provide suggestions and solutions for solving any problems family members are having after listening to what each person has to say.

Counselors can act as intermediaries between family members having a dispute. By doing this, they will have more of a chance to help the family assess the situation and try to solve the dispute than if the family members continue to battle it out at home. This can be very helpful if there are multiple children, either teens or others, in the family, as they usually have the hardest time in their adjustment. Teens are at such a trying stage of life already that if they suddenly find themselves having to live with another teen, problems can arise. Very often two people fighting, especially teens, become stubborn and selfish and cannot see the other person's side unless it is shown to them through the skills of an intermediary.

Participating in family therapy can be a useful experience for newly blended families. In this safe environment, each family member can express their feelings as well as learn how everyone else is feeling.

It is also beneficial to continue going as a group to the counseling sessions over a long period of time. This way the counselor becomes the family's friend and adviser and has the chance to watch the family dynamic develop and improve with time. After a while, the counselor will be able to assess the progress that has been made and advise the family members on how to continue working together and solving their problems.

Consider Your Parents' Happiness

As a teenager, transitioning to a blended family certainly will not be easy. However, there are several things to consider aside from the fact that a blended family may not be exactly what you had in mind for your life.

Teens often forget that the life changes that affect them affect their parents as well. If you have experienced the divorce of your parents, it was undoubtedly hard on you. Try taking a minute to think about your parents' feelings, too. Even if they were in an unhappy relationship and it was in their best interest to get divorced, the breakup of a marriage is still extremely painful. Suddenly they are single, and this time as parents. That is no easy task.

Zach groaned when his father told him that Heather would be his new stepmother. Zach was not Heather's biggest fan. However, when Zach began staying with his dad and Heather on weekends and for a few weeks in the summer, he realized how calm his dad was now. Zach loved his mother more than anything, and he wished his parents were still together. But when he thought back to all the fights his parents had every night, he realized how much

Even if you don't particularly like your parent's new spouse, try to keep an open mind. Does your parent seem a lot happier now? If so, there must be something to like about your new stepparent.

happier his dad was being married to Heather. His dad was a good guy, he deserved to be happy, so Zach put his feelings aside and gave Heather a chance.

Although as a teenager you are dealing with seemingly endless problems, take a moment to think like an adult and put yourself in your parents' shoes. Try to realize that they are dealing with major changes as well. It may help to look at them as people and not just as your parents. The popular phrase "Parents are people, too" says it best. Just as you need someone to talk to about your anxieties, so do they.

In particular, try to think about this when your parents begin dating again and perhaps meet someone they like. Don't they deserve to be happy, too? Very often a divorced person finds solace in talking to another divorced person and hearing how he or she handled problems. Just as you can relate to your peers and friends, your parents can relate to theirs. For a parent to find another parent who has been through a divorce or who understands what it is like to lose a spouse can be extremely comforting.

Keep a Strong Bond

Even while trying to adjust to the blended family, there will always be a need for you to spend time alone with your natural parent. The bond between you and your parent is still very important. Having special time alone with your parent will help you in your adjustment to the blended family. It will provide an outlet for you to speak privately with your parent and express any feelings and anxieties you may be having.

Kwame was in the fifth grade when his mother married Andre. Along with gaining a stepfather, Kwame also got two stepbrothers and, later, a half sister. After a little while, Kwame felt like everyone fit together like a regular happy family. But once a week, Kwame's mother made a date with him to get an ice cream cone after school, just the two of them. It made Kwame feel special to have that time alone with his mom.

In addition, this time together can be an assurance that you have not lost your parent during the formation of the blended family. Not only do teenagers often resent their stepparent for being the new person their parent relies on, but they may also fear that their parent is going to be "taken away" from them by their stepparent. Spending time alone together will allow you and your parent to have a little time out just to enjoy being together, and it will reassure you that your parent is not being "taken away."

Ask your natural parent if the two of you can schedule an activity every now and then, without any other family members. Having this one-on-one time can remind you that your parent is still devoted to you.

The Benefits of a Blended Family

Blended families are full of positive elements, although you may not see them right away. It is important to note that having a stepparent does not mean that anyone expects you to forget about your mom or dad who does not live with you anymore.

Being in a blended family simply means that you have more people in your life. There may be more siblings who are close to your age and can ultimately turn into new friends. There may also be more grandparents, aunts, uncles, and cousins. The addition of these people to your life can add not only to the number of people in your family but to the warmth and happiness within the family as well. Remember, you have not lost the people in your old family—you have just gained an extended family.

GLOSSARY

ADOLESCENCE The time of development between puberty and adulthood; the teenage years.

BLENDED FAMILY A family that forms when two adults get married and at least one of them has a child or children from a previous marriage; also known as a stepfamily.

DEFENSE MECHANISM A mental coping technique to avoid conflict.

DIVORCE The termination of a marriage.

HALF SIBLING The child of your natural parent and stepparent.

INTERMEDIARY Person who acts as a go-between to resolve a conflict or bring about an agreed-upon resolution.

NATURAL FAMILY The family that exists before divorce and remarriage, usually made up of parents and their biological children.

NATURAL PARENT A parent who is biologically related to you.

STEPPARENT The person your parent marries, either after your natural parents have divorced or one parent has died.

STEPSIBLING The child of the person your parent marries.

FOR MORE INFORMATION

American Association for Marriage and Family Therapy
112 South Alfred Street
Alexandria, VA 22314-3061
(703) 838-9808
Website: http://www.aamft.org
This organization offers support and suggestions for seeking
family therapy to cope with divorce and blended families.

American Academy of Pediatrics
141 Northwest Point Boulevard
Elk Grove Village, IL 60007-1098
(800) 433-9026
Website: http://www.aap.org
The American Academy of Pediatrics researches and advocates for health care for children, including mental health care and guidance.

Childhelp USA Hotline
(800) 422-4453
This hotline is available in English and Spanish for young people in crisis.

Children's Defense Fund (CDF)
25 E Street NW
Washington, DC 20001
(800) 233-1200
Website: http://www.childrensdefense.org
CDF provides a voice for all the children of America who cannot vote, lobby, or speak for themselves. CDF educates the nation about the needs of children and encourages

preventive investments before they get sick, drop out of school, get into trouble, or suffer family breakdown.

Children's Rights Council
1296 Cronson Boulevard, Suite 3086
Crofton, MD 21114
(301) 459-1220
Website: http://www.crckids.org

The Children's Rights Council is dedicated to helping divorced, separated, and never married parents remain actively and responsibly involved in their child's life. Parents can join local groups to help them deal with their situation.

Erika's Lighthouse
897 1/2 Green Bay Road
Winnetka, IL 60093
(847) 386-6481
Website: http://www.erikaslighthouse.org
This organization educates and empowers teens to take charge of their mental health.

Girl Talk
3490 Piedmont Road NE, Suite 1104
Atlanta, GA 30305
Website: http://www.mygirltalk.org/GirlTalkResources/
ParentandTeacherResources.aspx
Girl Talk is a peer mentoring program that enlists high school-aged young women to mentor middle school girls. Mentors help these girls deal with issues they're facing during their formative teenage years. These relationships help develop

confidence, leadership skills, and compassion, and teach the girls how to face life's problems.

Rainbows Headquarters
1007 Church Street, Suite 408
Evanston, IL 60201
(847) 952-1770
Website: http://www.rainbows.org
Rainbows offers support for all youth who are dealing with loss, including divorce. Rainbows features a network of trained facilitators to guide young people through their grief.

Stepfamily Foundation
310 West 85th Street, Suite 1B
New York, NY 10024
(212) 877-3244
Website: http://www.stepfamily.org
This nonprofit organization provides counseling for the stepfamily/blended family, divorce counseling, remarriage counseling, and stepfamily certification seminars.

Websites

Because of the changing nature of Internet links, Rosen Publishing has developed an online list of websites related to the subject of this book. This site is updated regularly. Please use this link to access the list:

http://www.rosenlinks.com/DIV/blend

FOR FURTHER READING

Baker, Amy J. L., and Katherine Andre. *Getting Through My Parents' Divorce*. Oakland, CA: Instant Help Books, 2015.

Bergin, Rory M., and Jared Meyer. *Frequently Asked Questions About Divorce*. New York, NY: Rosen Publishing, 2012.

Bryfonski, Dedria. *Child Custody*. Farmington Hills, MI: Greenhaven Press, 2011.

Espejo, Roman. *Custody and Divorce*. Detroit, MI: Greenhaven Press, 2013.

Gay, Kathlyn. *Divorce: The Ultimate Teen Guide*. Lanham, MD: Rowman & Littlefield, 2014.

Iorizzo, Carrie. *Divorce and Blended Families*. St. Catharines, ON, Canada: Crabtree Publishing Company, 2013.

Kavanaugh, Dorothy. *Hassled Girl?: Girls Dealing with Feelings*. Berkeley Heights, NJ: Enslow Publishers, 2014.

McLaughlin, Jerry, and Katherine E. Krohn. *Dealing with Your Parents' Divorce*. New York, NY: Rosen Publishing, 2016.

Peterman, Rosie L., Jared Meyer, and Charlie Quill. *Divorce and Stepfamilies*. New York, NY: Rosen Publishing, 2013.

Stewart, Sheila, and Rae Simons. *I Live in Two Homes: Adjusting to Divorce and Remarriage*. Broomall, PA: Mason Crest Publishers, 2011.

INDEX

school psychologists, talking
to, 14, 37
social workers, talking to, 37
stepmothers, stereotypes of,
15, 16–17
stepparent
feelings of guilt for liking, 12,
35–36, 44
resentment of, 10, 33–34, 42
what to call, 36–37
stepsiblings, adapting to,
17–19, 20
support groups, 39–41

U

unconditional love, 45

About the Authors

Becky Lenarki was employed as a social worker for thirty years. She enjoys spending time with her grandchildren, who are part of a happily blended family.

Julie Leibowitz is an editor based in New York.

Photo Credits

Cover Golden Pixels LLC/Shutterstock.com; back cover, pp. 4–5 © iStockphoto.com/jsmith; p. 5 Studio-Annika/iStock/Thinkstock; p. 9 James Pauls/E+/Getty Images; p. 10 Image Source/Photodisc/Getty Images; p. 13 Rob Marmion/Shutterstock; p. 17 © AF archive/Alamy Stock Photo; p. 18 sturti/E+/Getty Images; p. 21 © iStockphoto.com/FamVeld; p. 22 Susan Chiang/E+/Getty Images; p. 25 Purestock/Getty Images; p. 26 Monkey Business Images/Shutterstock.com; pp. 28–29 Steve Mason/Photodisc/Thinkstock; pp. 30–31 Purestock/Thinkstock; pp. 34–35 Yellow Dog Productions/The Image Bank/Getty Images; pp. 38–39 pixelheadphoto/Shutterstock.com; pp. 40–41 Tom Merton/Caiaimage/Getty Images; pp. 42–43 Stephen Simpson/Iconica/Getty Images; pp. 46–47 Jack Hollingsworth/Photodisc/Thinkstock; p. 50 Pamela Moore/E+/Getty Images; p. 52 Blend Images/Shutterstock.com; pp. 54–55 Fuse/Getty Images; interior pages textured background chungking/Shutterstock.com.

Designer: Nicole Russo; Editor: Christine Poolos; Photo Researcher: Sherri Jackson